CAR
SCIENCE

DK Publishing

DK

LONDON, NEW YORK,
MELBOURNE, MUNICH, and DELHI

Senior editor Ben Morgan
Editors Wendy Horobin, Deborah Lock, Alexander Cox
Senior designers Claire Patane, Karen Hood
Designers Laura Roberts, Sadie Thomas, Hedi Gutt
Illustrators Chris Longhurst, Alex Bec, Richard Burgess
Production controller Pip Tinsley
Production editor Siu Chan
Jacket designers Karen Hood, Natalie Godwin
Jacket editor Mariza O'Keeffe
Design manager Rachael Foster
Publishing manager Bridget Giles
Creative director Jane Bull
Publisher Mary Ling

Consultants Dr Jon Woodcock, Chris Woodford, Chris Longhurst

First published in United States in 2008 by DK Publishing
375 Hudson Street, New York, New York 10014

A CIP catalogue record for this book is available from the Library of Congress

ISBN: 978-0-7566-5025-4

Color reproduction by Alta Image, Great Britain
Printed and bound by Hung Hing, China

Discover more at
www.dk.com

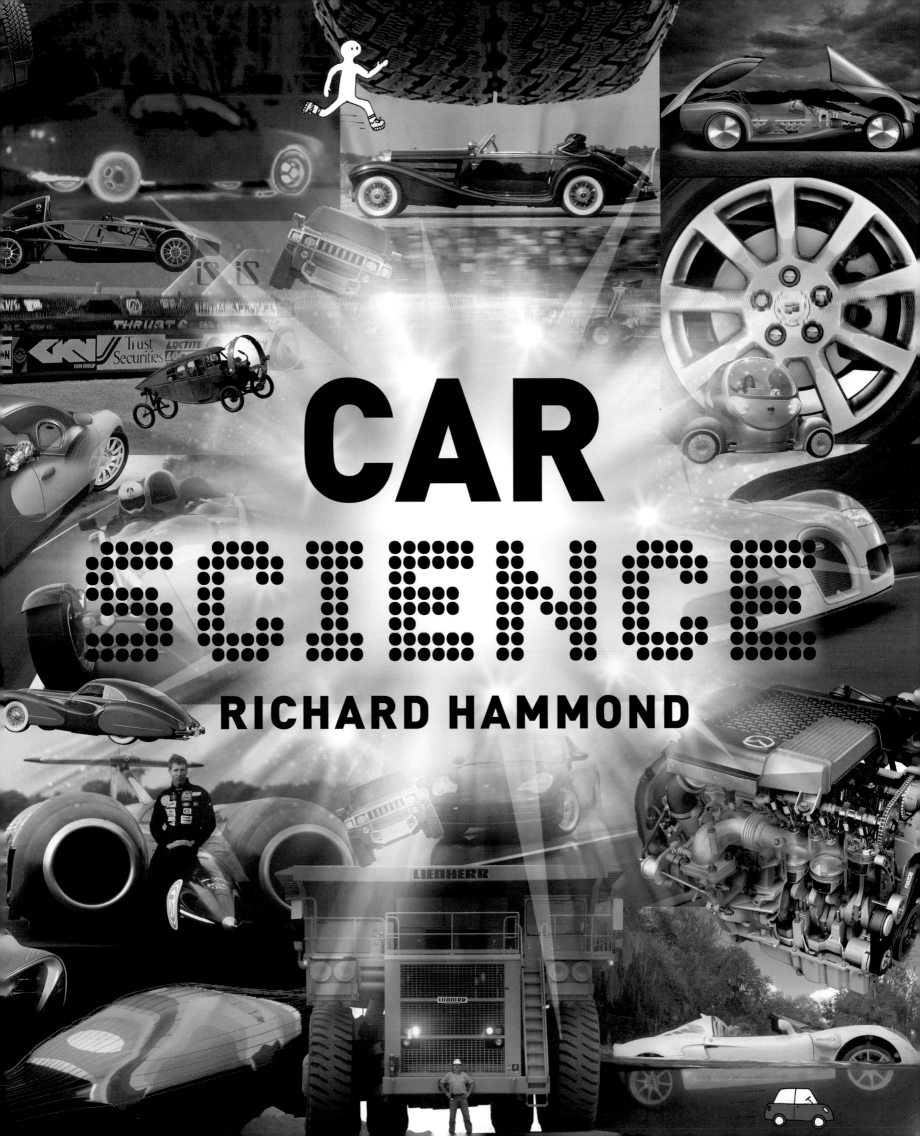

CAR SCIENCE

RICHARD HAMMOND

Contents

1 Power

2 Speed

Introduction

Cars are crammed full of science. How fast they go, how quickly they can stop, and how furiously they can go around a corner are all down to science. And that's a good thing, because two things that I really love are cars and science. How convenient, two of my favorite things all in one.

I know people who can tell the difference between a 1985 and 1986 Ford Fiesta from 500 yards in a snowstorm and who can remember the part number for a 1965 Morris Minor handbrake cable, but what they can't explain to me is the difference between power and torque.

Things like this are very useful for us to know. Lewis Hamilton and his buddies in Formula 1 don't just drive their cars faster and faster until they crash and then remember to go a little bit slower the next time; they understand what makes their cars stick to the road like an octopus wearing velcro shoes on a carpet. And because they understand the science involved, they can help their engineers make the cars go even faster and, therefore, win races and become rich and famous.

Lots of people driving on the road don't really understand the science in their cars. If they did they wouldn't drive so close to the car in front on the highway because

they'd know about things like inertia and momentum, and would know that if the car in front stops dead they won't be able to stop in time. And if they knew a lot about the science of cars they'd know that stopping suddenly from 70 mph (110 km/h) involves a lot of forces. And tears and bruises.

It's a huge subject, so we've been very sensible and split this book into four chapters: Power, Speed, Handling, and Technology. Each chapter covers everything you need to know to be a real driving expert. How a turbocharger works, how gasoline is made; we'll look inside gearboxes and learn why a Formula 1 car's brakes glow pink when it's stopping. And at the end, we'll look at the kind of cars that we might be driving in the future.

Throughout the book we'll be meeting one of the world's first experts, Sir Isaac Newton (you can't miss him, he's an old-looking geezer with a crazy dress sense and a massive wig). Most of us know that one day an apple fell on Isaac's head and he realized that gravity existed, but he came up with lots of other brainy ideas and theories, too, most of which are very important to cars.

We know you'll learn a lot, and we hope you enjoy doing so.

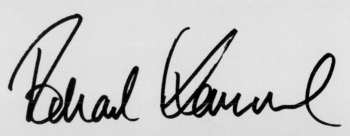

Power **is one of the most exciting words in the English language**. Politicians love it and so do car enthusiasts, because it makes our cars go fast. And driving a fast car is much more fun than sitting in the Houses of Representatives arguing about the level of farm subsidies.

So where does power come from? It's all about converting energy from one form (fuel) into another (movement). It's really very simple, as you're about to find out.

Some people are never satisfied with what they have and want even more, so we'll look at ways of making more of what we call "horsepower." Like making engines bigger, or making a small engine more powerful by cramming more fuel into it.

Incidentally, why on Earth is it called horsepower? ...

Power

Goodbye horse!

The history of the car is really the history of **FUEL.** Ever since people invented the *wheel*, they've tried powering vehicles with everything from donkeys to fryer fat. For a long time, *horse power* was the best option. The first true automobiles didn't appear until the invention of the **GASOLINE** engine.

Muscle power

Stone Age motoring 10,000 BC

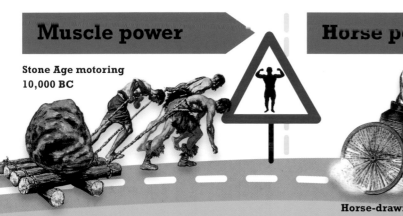

Horse-drawn carriage

Horse power

Coal power

During the 1700s, inventors in England discovered how to harness the energy in coal to make vehicles move, doing away with the need for horses. These "steam engines" used a coal fire to boil water and make steam, which then drove pistons to push the wheels around. But all the water, coal, and steel made the vehicles much too heavy to run on normal ground, so they had to roll along steel rails—and so trains were invented. Steam trains were great for hauling huge loads, but small personal cars remained no more than a dream.

In the beginning, muscle power was the only way of traveling or carrying stuff around on land. Heavy objects had to be dragged, which was back-breaking work, even if you used a few logs to make the going easier. It was a long, long time before wheels were invented, around 4000 BC in what's now Iraq. It wasn't simply a matter of chopping logs into round slices—someone also had to invent the tricky axles that go through the middle. There was one handy alternative to muscle power: water. Wherever there were rivers, people could use them as roads by traveling on rafts, canoes, or other types of boats—the oldest form of transportation in the world.

Around 4000 BC, the fearsome warriors of Mongolia tamed wild horses and then rode into neighboring countries on murderous raids. The horse soon caught on everywhere, and it wasn't long before someone put horses and wheels together and came up with horse-drawn carts and carriages. Animal power remained the only form of transportation on land for more than 5,000 years.

Steam engine, 1808

Solar power

In one way or another, all cars are powered by secondhand solar energy. So why not simply use the Sun's energy directly? The answer is that the energy in raw sunshine just isn't sufficiently concentrated. In contrast, fuels like gas contain huge amounts of secondhand solar energy concentrated into a small space. Nevertheless, some engineers are trying to build working solar cars. These experimental vehicles are

Harnessing the Sun

What do all the different power sources on these pages have in common? Believe it or not, all of them supply energy that came originally from the Sun. Nearly all the energy we use on Earth comes from the Sun, and it usually comes to us via plants. Gasoline, diesel, and coal are called "fossil fuels" because they come from fossilized plants.

Battery power

In the late 1800s there was a race to invent the "horseless carriage"— a small, lightweight vehicle that didn't need rails. Coal was too heavy to use for fuel, so people tried other things, including natural gas, gunpowder, and something we now think of as modern: batteries. For a while, batteries seemed to be the answer—by 1897 New York City had a fleet of electric taxis, and in 1899 the world land-speed record of 68 mph (109 km/h) was set in an electric car. But the batteries were heavy and cumbersome relative to the power they supplied, and they burned out if you tried to go fast.

Gas power

The real breakthrough in the race to create the horseless carriage came when a German inventor, Nikolaus Otto, stole an ingenious idea from a French rival, Joseph Lenoir—and then improved it. Lenoir had built an "internal combustion engine," so named because it burned fuel inside a metal engine rather than on an open fire. Lenoir's engine used natural gas, but in 1876 Otto adapted it to burn gasoline. It worked brilliantly—and so began the age of cars. Soon gas cars built by the likes of Henry Ford in the US were all over the world.

The future...

So what's next? Gasoline and diesel, which have been the driving world's favorite sources of power for a century, could be on the way out, and the next big fuel might be hydrogen. Hydrogen is a clean fuel because it doesn't directly cause pollution: the only waste product it makes is water. And a clever device called a fuel cell can use hydrogen to make electricity, which can then be used to drive the wheels of electric cars. But there are a few snags to iron out before hydrogen takes over: like finding ways of making it, storing it, and delivering it to cars.

Electric car, 1896

Henry Ford in
Model N Ford, 1905

Ford Focus

Honda FCX Clarity
fuel-cell car

powered by large solar panels that produce only a trickle of electricity. To make the most of their weak power, the cars are ultrastreamlined and lightweight, with room for only one person, who has to lie down. And they aren't very fast. And if you don't live in a very sunny country like Australia, they aren't really an awful lot of use.

Just like a **human body**, a **car** can't do anything without ...

ENERGY

You might think that the way cars work has nothing in common with the human body, but you'd be very wrong. When it comes to the way cars and bodies use **ENERGY**, they do just the same job (but don't put spaghetti in your car).

Human body

The chemical wizardry that frees energy from food inside our bodies produces heat. Heat is invisible to the human eye, but with a special camera we can photograph it. This thermogram of an ice skater shows her body is much warmer than her chilly surroundings. The bare skin of her face is losing heat especially fast.

Spot the difference:

A **body** gets energy from **food** molecules. These are made of long chains of carbon atoms joined together by plants. The Sun's energy became trapped in the molecules as the plants constructed them.

Spaghetti

Inside a **body**, **food** molecules react with oxygen sucked in from the air. The reaction breaks down the bonds between carbon atoms and rearranges the atoms into new combinations. This frees the trapped energy. Oxygen and carbon atoms join to make carbon dioxide, which the **lungs** must breathe out.

The chemical energy freed from **food** molecules is converted into new forms of energy: heat and movement.

Cars and bodies are powered by the same basic equation:

 FUEL +  OXYGEN →

The energy that powers bodies and cars originally comes from the Sun as light energy. Plants convert light into chemical energy, which then becomes trapped when dead plants are turned into food or gasoline. The chemical energy is then changed into kinetic energy (movement energy) by a car's engine or a human body. Energy never really gets "used up"—it just keeps getting changed from one form to another.

Light energy   Chemical energy   Chemical energy again   Kinetic energy

 Car

A **car** gets energy from **fuel** molecules. These are made of long chains of carbon atoms joined together by plants. The Sun's energy became trapped in the molecules as the plants constructed them.

Gas

Inside a **car**, **fuel** molecules react with oxygen sucked in from the air. The reaction breaks down the bonds between carbon atoms and rearranges the atoms into new combinations. This frees the trapped energy. Oxygen and carbon atoms join to make carbon dioxide, which the **exhaust** must breathe out.

The chemical energy freed from **fuel** molecules is converted into new forms of energy: heat and movement.

The thermogram of a car shows heat leaking out of the engine bay. Car engines harness the explosive power of heat to drive their moving parts.

ENERGY +  CO$_2$ + WATER

What makes it GO?

If someone asks you to explain in three words how a car works, here's what to say ... 👉

... like a bike!

Of course, there are some differences between cars and bicycles—cars can't do very good wheelies, for instance. But when you look at the parts of a car that actually make the wheels go around, it all turns out to be surprisingly similar to your average bike. Let's take a closer look...

Pump action

On your BIKE ...

When you ride a bike, you power it by pumping your feet up and down vertically. The pedals are connected to the bike by levers called cranks, which turn the up-and-down motion into *rotation*, which is the kind of motion wheels need. The rotation gets fed to the wheels through the chain and gears. So: your legs go up and down, the wheels go around and around. That pushes you forward.

Gear

Crank

Pedal

The pistons in the engine pump up and down separately, but they're all joined together at the crankshaft. At the end of the crankshaft is a heavy metal wheel—a flywheel—that smooths the motion. The flywheel also helps keep things moving thanks to something called **inertia**. We'll find out a lot more about that later in the book.

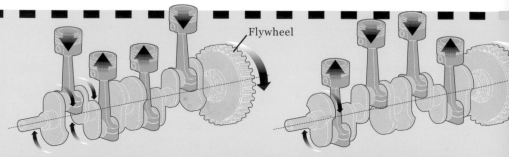

Flywheel

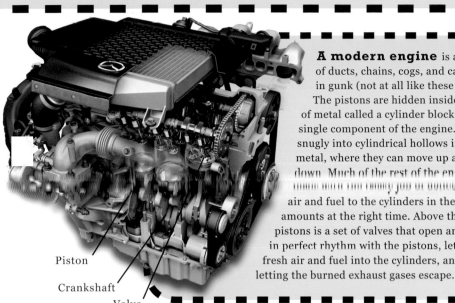

Piston
Crankshaft
Valve

A modern engine is a confusing mass of ducts, chains, cogs, and cables, all covered in gunk (not at all like these shiny pictures). The pistons are hidden inside a large chunk of metal called a cylinder block—the biggest single component of the engine. They fit snugly into cylindrical hollows in the metal, where they can move up and down. Much of the rest of the engine air and fuel to the cylinders in the right amounts at the right time. Above the pistons is a set of valves that open and close in perfect rhythm with the pistons, letting fresh air and fuel into the cylinders, and then letting the burned exhaust gases escape.

... and in your CAR

Now for the car engine. Deep inside it, hidden underneath the confusing mass of bits and pieces, is a row of metal cylinders called pistons that pump up and down, just like your feet on a bike. The pistons are joined to levers called cranks, which turn the up-and-down motion into rotation. As with a bike, the rotation is then fed to the wheels through the car's gears.

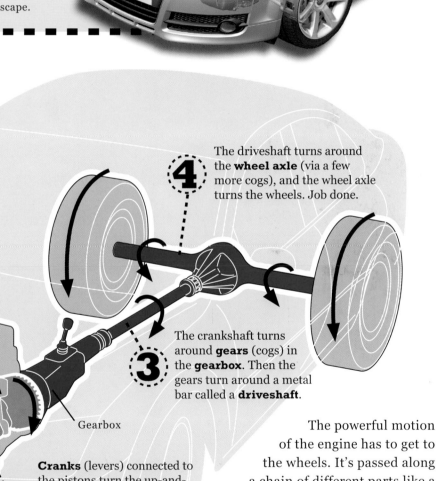

4 The driveshaft turns around the **wheel axle** (via a few more cogs), and the wheel axle turns the wheels. Job done.

3 The crankshaft turns around **gears** (cogs) in the **gearbox**. Then the gears turn around a metal bar called a **driveshaft**.

1 **Pistons** pump up and down like legs.

Gearbox

2 **Cranks** (levers) connected to the pistons turn the up-and-down motion into rotation, turning around something called the **crankshaft**.

The powerful motion of the engine has to get to the wheels. It's passed along a chain of different parts like a relay race, with all these parts spinning around powerfully. Together, these parts of a car make up what's called the **powertrain**.

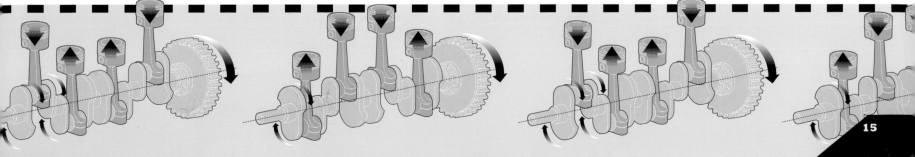

Fire power
The science of combustion

Combustion / noun
1: an act of burning.
2: a chemical reaction (oxidation) that makes heat and light.

As we've just seen, the pistons in an engine are the parts that do the pushing, like a cyclist's legs. Fine, but what pushes the pistons? The pictures on this page should give you a clue. The answer is the explosive power of FIRE. This is where a car stops being like the human body and starts getting a whole lot more interesting and a whole lot more powerful. The chemical reactions that power your muscles are slow and gentle, but the chemical reactions that power a car are fast and violent. The fuel doesn't just burn: it **explodes**. Hundreds of times *every second*.

CRASH BANG WALLOP!

What a picture! The stupendous force of a massive gas explosion sends two cars hurtling through the air like toys. Except this isn't actually possible. The explosion is completely fake—a stunt set up for a Hollywood movie. Cars can't explode like this: there just isn't enough oxygen in the fuel tank for the gas to burn that quickly.

What actually *is* fire?
Fire is a high-speed chemical reaction happening right before your eyes. Oxygen from the air reacts with energy-rich molecules (like the molecules in gasoline) to form new compounds that are given off as gases. The energy that was trapped in the fuel molecules escapes as heat and light, making the gases glow: a flame. The heat also makes the gases expand, and that can happen violently: an explosion. If you trap the exploding gas in a confined space, it creates a pushing force. And that's what pushes the pistons in an engine.

WARNING
EXPLOSIONS

internal combustion

Every second about **300** tiny explosions happen in the engine, each one burning up just a *thousandth of a teaspoon* of gas. These microdoses of gas are squirted into the cylinders as a spray and set alight by carefully timed electric sparks. The explosions happen right inside the engine's cylinders, on top of the pistons, and the **BLAST FORCE** pushes the pistons down. The crankshaft then swings around and pushes the pistons back up for the next stage in the cycle. Each piston makes 4 "strokes" (up or down movements) for every bang. The whole cycle for just one piston is shown below.

The pistons fit snugly into hollow cylinders in a large block of metal—the engine block. Fuel burns inside the cylinders (that's why it's called an *internal combustion engine.*)

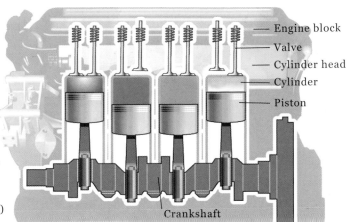

- Engine block
- Valve
- Cylinder head
- Cylinder
- Piston

Crankshaft

The FOUR-STROKE CYCLE

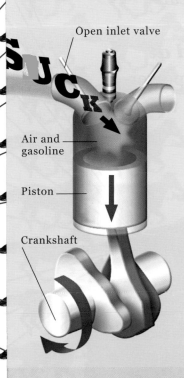

Open inlet valve

Air and gasoline

Piston

Crankshaft

Spark plug

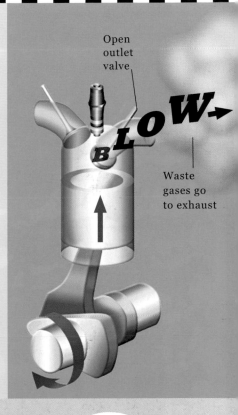

Open outlet valve

Waste gases go to exhaust

Suck (down stroke): The piston moves down, sucking in air through the inlet valve. A tiny squirt of gasoline is injected into the air. ①

Squeeze (up stroke): The inlet valve at the top closes, trapping everything inside. The piston moves up, squeezing the air and gasoline tightly together. ②

Bang (down stroke): When the piston reaches the top, a carefully timed spark sets fire to the gasoline. The gas burns explosively, forcing the piston back down. ③

Blow (up stroke): Finally, the piston moves back up and pushes the burned gases out of the outlet valve. These gases leave the car through the exhaust. ④

Revving it up

During one whole cycle of "suck, squeeze, bang, blow," the pistons move up and down twice, turning the crankshaft around twice as well. This all happens amazingly quickly. Next time you're in a car, look at the dashboard. Next to the speedometer is a smaller dial called the rev counter. It shows how fast the crankshaft is turning around, in revolutions per

minute (rpm). The numbers stand for thousands, so if the needle is on 5, the crankshaft is doing 5,000 rpm, which works out as 83 revolutions per second! When the driver puts his or her foot down, the engine spins even faster and the needle climbs. If the engine goes too fast, the needle crosses the "redline." At these high revs, the engine generates such powerful forces that it can damage itself.

SUPERPOWER

Option 1: Make the engine BIG

The bigger the engine, the more fuel it can swallow. The world's biggest truck is the Liebherr T282. It's the size of a small house and its engine is as big as a car. A typical car might take in 1.5 liters of air and gasoline with each cycle, but the engine in this monster takes in 78 liters. Which makes it pretty powerful. And it needs to be: its job is to haul vast heaps of mining rubble, and it weighs over 550 tons (500 metric tons) fully laden. **Big engines can generate enormous pulling power** for hauling loads, but there's a catch: they **weigh a lot**, which means they **slow the vehicle down**. The Liebherr has a top speed of only 40 mph (64 km/h) and a 0 to 60 time of never.

LIEBHERR

LIEBHERR
MINING POWER

For sale
$4 million

Top speed: 40 mph (64 km/h)

0–60 mph (0–97 km/h)**:** never

Miles per gallon: 0.3

Empty vehicle weight: 221 tons

Power: 3,500 horsepower

Power is all about burning fuel quickly, and you can make an engine do that in different ways. One way is to make the engine huge, so it can gulp in more fuel with each turn of the crankshaft. Another way is to make it spin faster. These two routes to superpower are used in very different kinds of vehicles.

Option 2: Make the engine *fast*

Top speed: 229 mph (369 km/h)

0–60 mph (97 km/h)**:** 2.45 seconds

Miles per gallon: 3

Empty vehicle weight: 0.6 tons

Power: 800–1,000 horsepower

Formula 1 cars have engines that **generate power by spinning fast.** An F1 car must be as **light as possible,** so its engine is kept small. With a capacity of only 2.4 liters, it's about the same size as the engine in a nice family car. But what it lacks in size it more than makes up for in revs. It can spin around at a ferocious 19,000 rpm, which is more than ten times faster than the Licbhcrr's sluggish 1,500 rpm. So what's the catch? Aside from screaming like a banshee, fast-revving engines wear out very quickly.

For sale
$6 million

Can you talk the torque?

Engineers compare the brute strength of different engines by measuring a mysterious thing called torque. It sounds complicated, but it's actually very simple: torque is just a twisting force. When you use a wrench to loosen a bolt, the wrench generates a torque on the bolt. The longer the wrench, the greater the torque. The pistons in a car generate torque on the crankshaft in the same way. As with the wrench, the bigger the pistons and the cranks, the greater the torque. The massive pistons in the dump truck engine produce a stupendous amount of torque,

which gives the truck enormous pulling power even when the engine is only idling. The Formula 1 car is the opposite. Its lightweight enginc has small pistons that produce little torque—barely more than a good production car. So to unleash the engine's full power, the driver has to rev it up to the max. The two routes to power can be summed up in a neat equation:

power = torque x revs

21

Step on the gas (or air)

Fuel on its own is useless—it won't burn and release energy unless you add the same magic ingredient that keeps you going: **OXYGEN.** And to get all the oxygen it needs, an engine must gulp in a truly vast quantity of air: about 9,000 times as much air by volume as gasoline. Your lungs breathe in about 6 liters of fresh air a minute, but a powerful car needs thousands of times as much.

25 liters of air per minute

75 liters of air per minute

3,000 liters of air per minute

Citroen C3

The accelerator pedal in a car is really an "air pedal." It works by opening a valve called the throttle, which lets more air into the engine, which also indirectly increases how much fuel enters the engine. With more fuel and air entering the engine, the explosions in the cyclinders become more forceful and the pistons are pushed harder, making the engine spin faster. The revs increase, and so the wheels spin faster too, making the car accelerate.

Power boosters

The reason big engines are more powerful than small engines is because they can hold more air. But you can also cram more air molecules into the cylinders by squeezing the air in more tightly. This is what superchargers and turbos do. These devices are basically air compressors that push more air into the cylinders, which in turn causes more fuel to be drawn in too. The result is more powerful explosions—and therefore a whole lot more torque to play with.

18,000 liters
of air
per minute

12,000
liters
of air
per minute

Bugatti Veyron

Formula 1 car

Superchargers
These are also called "blowers." Unlike a turbo, a supercharger is driven by a belt connected to the crankshaft. As the car speeds up, the supercharger makes a high-pitched whine that gets louder and louder—which is all part of the fun.

Turbochargers
Turbochargers are driven by hot air rushing out of the car's exhaust. Some types of turbo kick in suddenly as you rev up the engine, causing a sudden rush of speed and adrenaline.

Nitrous oxide
Nitrous oxide is a gas that breaks down inside the engine, boosting the amount of oxygen within the cylinders and making the combustion more powerful. It's often used in drag racing, but some people equip ordinary cars with nitrous kits to boost horsepower.

Piston power

As we've seen, the pistons in an engine do the same job as your legs when you're riding a bike. But you only have two legs. Imagine how much more powerful your bike would be if you had four or eight legs instead (though saying that, you'd need a pretty weird bike). Well, cars can have as many pistons as they like, within reason. And the number and the shape in which they're arranged both have a big influence on the power and personality of the car.

This is tricky with 11 legs!

Single

Engines with a single cylinder don't have enough power for cars, but they're fine for lawnmowers and mopeds. Because there are no other pistons to smooth out the bangs, they produce a lot of vibration.

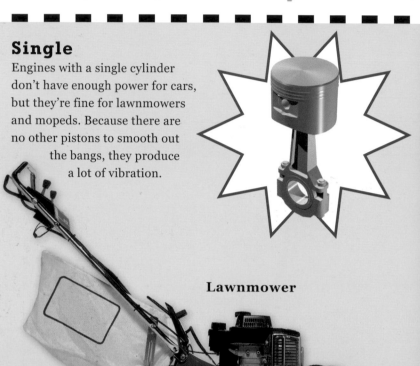

Lawnmower

V twin

Motorcycles tend to have 1–4 cylinders, but the Harley-Davidson has two arranged in a V. The pistons are large and don't move up and down very quickly. As a result, the Harley engine makes a distinctive *thump thump* noise that gives the bike lots of character. The engine shakes a lot, but that's part of the character, too.

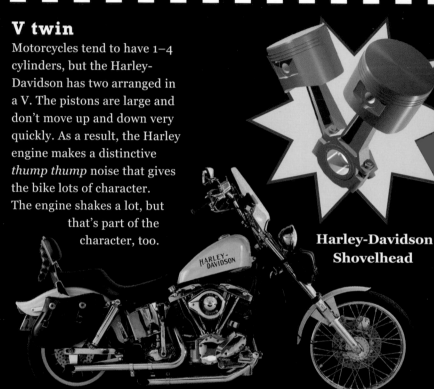

Harley-Davidson
Shovelhead

Straight 5

Straight 6 engines are very well balanced, but they're long and difficult to fit under the hood. The answer is to use a straight 5 instead. Not quite as smooth, but smoother than a straight 4. And they usually sound kind of deep and gruff, which is pretty nice, actually.

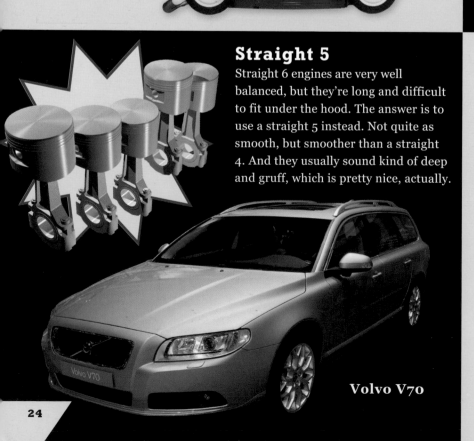

Volvo V70

V6

Instead of arranging six cylinders in a line you can put three on each side of a V. This makes a nice compact engine. A V6 is not quite as smooth as a straight 6 but has heaps of character and sounds very nice.

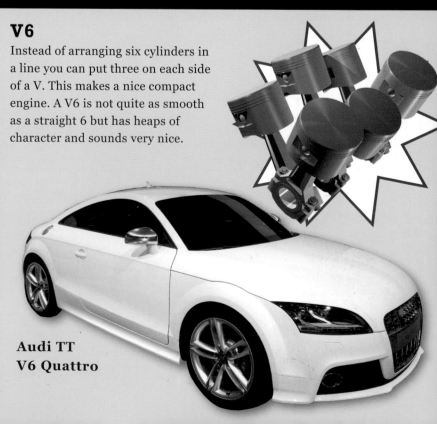

Audi TT
V6 Quattro

Capacity

The amount of air an engine can fit into all its cylinders at once is called **engine capacity**, and it's a good clue to the engine's power. It's measured in liters, so when someone says their car is a "two liter whatever" or a "something one-point-eight," they're telling you how much air their car's engine can hold.

Shape

The **cylinders** in an engine are arranged to fire in pairs or one after the other, which helps the engine run more smoothly. The shape of their arrangement also matters. In simple engines the cylinders are lined up, but this can magnify vibrations. Better to arrange them in opposite pairs, so they cancel each other out, or in a **V-shape.**

Straight 4

Most small family cars have straight (in-line) four-cylinder engines, usually up to about 2.0 liters in size. They're quite smooth, compact, and do a very good job. They do sound a bit boring though.

Ford Fiesta

Flat 4

The famous Beetle used a flat 4 engine. These are often called boxer engines because the pistons move like boxers' fists. One of the advantages of a flat 4 is that they can be mounted low in the car, which keeps the weight low down—good for handling. Flat engines make a very distinctive noise, especially when they're made with even more cylinders. Porsche's 911 has a flat 6, and Ferrari even made a flat 12.

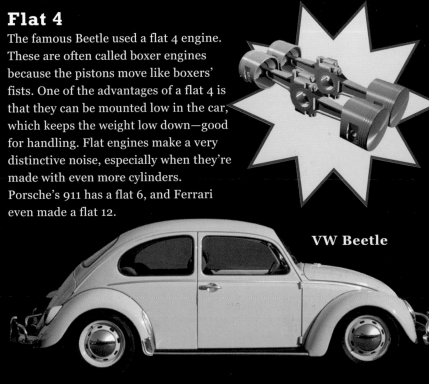

VW Beetle

V8

Car enthusiasts love V8s. They're big—usually over 3.5 liters—and powerful. But it's the noise that gets everybody excited, especially if the car's mufflers aren't very effective. A big V8 is almost like a living thing: it shakes and growls, and when you rev it the hairs on the back of your neck stand up.

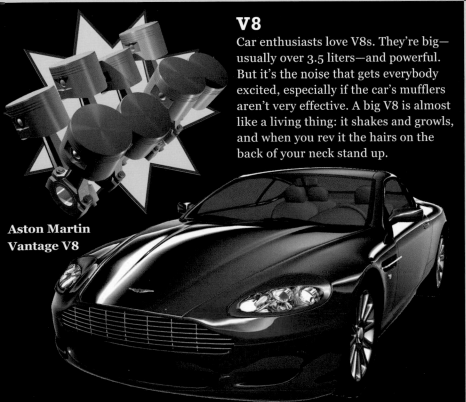

Aston Martin Vantage V8

Wankel Rotary

The rotary engine is very interesting. The pistons are triangular and move around inside an odd-shaped cylinder. Only Mazda uses these engines. They're very smooth, compact, and produce a lot of power. Without muffling they're incredibly loud, with a unique sound like carpet being torn. They also tend to be a bit thirsty for fuel.

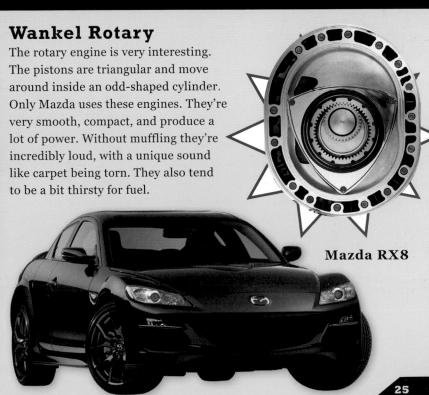

Mazda RX8

Bugatti Veyron

$1.7 million o.n.o.

Top speed:
253 mph (407 km/h)

0–60 mph: 2.46 sec
(0–97 km/h)

Engine: 8-liter W16 with
4 turbochargers

Power:
1,001 brake horsepower

Miles per gallon: 12
(normal) 2.5 mpg at full throttle

MONSTER ENGINE

Everything about the Bugatti Veyron is mind-boggling, including its price. Let's start with the engine: a 1,001-brake-horsepower monster that takes up a massive space in the center of the car. We've already seen how the pistons and crankshaft are laid out in an engine, and how some engines have only one piston and some have as many as eight. Well, the Veyron has 16 pistons and two crankshafts, with the pistons arranged in a W shape. Volkswagen (which owns Bugatti) built the engine by using parts from two of its 4.0-liter V8 engines, which is why the Veyron has a monster 8.0 liter capacity.

The 16 cylinders pump up and down in a coordinated cycle that makes the engine luxuriously smooth.

The Veyron's huge engine is connected to all four wheels (four-wheel drive), allowing the car to put all its power down without spinning them.

The MONSTER ENGINE with a beast of a price tag

We've seen how a turbocharger is used to cram more air (and hence more fuel) into an engine to increase the power—well, the Veyron has four of them. In fact, the Veyron has more of everything, including gears, of which it has seven. The gearbox is semiautomatic: it's like a conventional manual gearbox except that the clutches (yes, it has two) are operated automatically and the gears are engaged by flicking paddles on the steering wheel, like those on a Formula 1 car. When driving at 250 mph (402 km/h) it's quite a good idea to have good brakes. The Veyron has. The brake disks are made of carbon fiber and the front ones are squeezed by pads operated by eight pistons (most cars have only four). Bugatti says that the Veyron will come to a stop from **249 mph** (401 km/h) in under **10 seconds**. Hold on to your hat!

When its speed hits 137 mph (220 km/h), the Veyron's body lowers automatically to reduce air pressure under the car.

The streamlined shape allows air to flow smoothly over the surface.

Aerodynamics

Most vehicles that go faster than 250 mph (402 km/h) are called airplanes. As you can see, the Veyron is clearly a car. To stop the car from taking off at top speed like a plane, the Veyron's designers had to get the car's shape exactly right so that the wind pushes it down onto the road, creating "downforce." You can find out more about downforce on page 50.

The rear spoiler creates nearly half a ton of downforce to press the car onto the road.

Getting in GEAR

Why do you need gears?

The gears on a bike allow your legs to pump up and down at a comfortable speed all the time, even though the speed of the wheels changes enormously. A car's gears do exactly the same job (think of the pistons as legs). And just like a bike's gears, a car's gears can magnify torque—giving the wheels the powerful force they need to climb hills or get you going in the first place.

What are gears?

Gears are simply cogs—wheels with teeth. If you connect a small gear to a big gear with ten times as many teeth, the small gear will make ten turns for every one turn of the big gear. Now connect the small gear to the car's engine and the big gear to the wheels. Bingo! You've solved the problem of getting a fast-revving engine to turn the wheels slowly.

One engine, many cars

Using gears is like having many cars in one. You change gear to help your engine match the driving conditions, using your engine's power to create either lots of torque (to start moving or climb hills) or lots of speed (for highway cruising).

20%

From engine

1st gear

It takes huge force to get a car moving. In 1st gear, the wheels turn slowly but with masses of torque—ideal to get the car moving.

From engine
To wheels

2nd gear

Once you're moving, you need a bit more speed and a bit less torque. Choose 2nd gear: the wheels can now spin faster. But they still have plenty of torque—handy if you need a burst of acceleration.

From engine
To wheels

1st gear

Oh dear—you've come to a steep hill and slowed right down. You now need a lot more torque at the wheels again for the car to pull itself uphill. Back down to first gear please.

Axles turn wheels

Driveshaft carries power from engine

Inner wheel goes shorter distance and slower

Differential

Outer wheel goes farther and faster

Differential gears

There's a second, mini-gearbox tucked between the wheels. Shaped like a pumpkin, it's called a differential, and its main job is to help you go around corners. When a car rounds a bend, the outer wheels have to travel farther than the inner ones, so they have to turn faster. The cogs in the differential let a car's inner and outer wheels turn at different speeds. This is great for normal driving but there's a snag. If one wheel loses grip by riding into slippery mud or getting stuck in the air, the differential will let it spin like crazy and waste all the power. Off-roaders get around this problem by using clever differentials that direct power to whichever wheel has got the best grip.

Gears in the differential

Inside the gearbox

A car's gearbox contains pairs of cogs of varying sizes. One row sits on a shaft driven by the engine, and the others sit on a shaft that drives the wheels. At any moment, only one pair is clamped firmly to the rotating shafts and therefore carrying the engine's power. By using the gearshift, you can choose which pair does the job: a big cog connected to a little cog, a little cog connected to a big cog, or something in between.

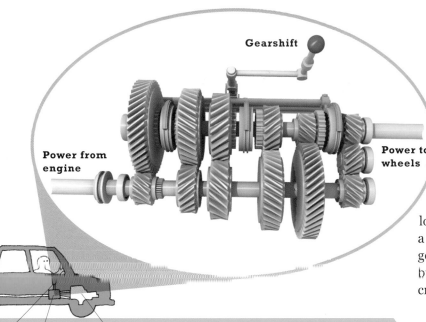

Gearshift

Power from engine

Power to wheels

Gearshift · Gearbox · Engine

Feel the force

As well as changing the speed at which a car's spinning parts are spinning, gears change the turning force—the torque. When a car is in a low gear (1st or 2nd), the wheels turn around slowly but with lots of torque—ideal for pulling a car uphill. When the car is in a high gear (3rd or 4th), the wheels spin fast but with little torque, which is fine for cruising at speed along highways.

40

60

2nd gear

Heading downhill, you don't really need any torque because gravity is doing all the work. But stay in a low gear anyway because it's safer—it will stop the wheels from spinning too quickly.

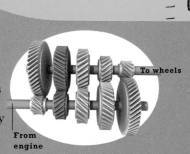

To wheels

From engine

3rd gear

Back on the straight, you can accelerate. Switch to 3rd, which allows your wheels to spin a lot faster.

To wheels

From engine

4th gear

You hit the highway. Now you want the wheels to spin fast rather than with lots of torque so choose 4th or higher.

To wheels

From engine

MAKE A SPUD GEARBOX

You will need:
- A thick piece of cardboard (an old carboard box is perfect)
- Toothpicks or sharp pencils
- Pastry cutters of various sizes (but with roughly the same sized teeth) or a table knife
- A few potatoes of different sizes (as round as possible)

1. Cut slices about ¼ in (0.5 cm) thick from the middle of each potato. You want your slices to be as round as possible. Use a small jar lid as a guide to help you trim them to a more circular shape.

2. Press out some "gears" of different sizes using the pastry cutters, or cut equal-sized notches around the edges of the potato circles.

3. Mount your gears onto the cardboard by pushing the toothpicks or pencils through the potato slices. Arrange the gears so their teeth mesh together. If you turn one wheel, you should find the others turn, too. If you make your gears the same size, they should all turn at the same speed.

4. Experiment with gears of different sizes. Try to turn a small gear with a big one—the smaller one should turn faster because it has fewer teeth. If you turn a large gear with a smaller one, the larger wheel should turn more slowly.

5. Don't worry if your gearbox doesn't work. You can always fry it to make fries and eat it for dinner!

Fantastic. We've dug a hole in the ground, found some oil, and we've turned it into gasoline. We've also designed a really amazing engine that's got more horsepower than the Kentucky Derby. Let's go fast.

But hold on, because there's more to going fast than just power. For starters, there's this thing called drag—the force of the air holding you back—and it's not good news for speed. Then there's weight: too much of it will slow you down even more, as you'd find out if you tried running with a kitchen table strapped to your back.

Lots of different forces are involved in the science of speed, and to break records we need to understand them. Race-car drivers, who go fast for a living, really need to understand the science of speed because otherwise they'll be slow. And then they're called losers.

speed

Ariel Atom

Despite appearances, this car is fully finished. The Ariel Atom's designer wanted to build a car that had the bare minimum of bodywork, giving it a fantastic power to weight ratio for great acceleration, and putting all its lovely mechanical parts on view. You don't commute to work in the Atom. It's for country driving on sunny days and blasting around race tracks faster than a Ferrari.

Pushrod-operated shock absorbers at the front and back give the Atom the dynamic handling of a race car.

Acceleration: 0–60 in 2.7 seconds
(similar to a Formula 1 car)

Weight: 1,005 lb (456 kg)
(half the weight of a compact car)

Power: 300 horsepower
(more than twice the power of a Mini)

There's not much bodywork on an Atom, which saves weight and allows easy access for adjustments. Panels are made of a woven fiber composite that is strong and light.

A steel roll bar around the air intake protects the driver's head if the car overturns in an accident. The tubular steel chassis is very strong and also protects the occupants. Looks great, too.

The air intake mounted behind the driver draws in hundreds of liters of air every second to feed a supercharged Honda engine that can power the car to a zippy top speed of 155 mph (250 km/h).

Twin exhausts

Rear engine

The Atom's four-cylinder engine is mounted behind the driver, as in a race car. This is the view you'll have if you're on a race track with one.

Lightweight alloy wheels

Bucket seats

Tubular chassis

One of the most unusual features of the Atom is its open frame construction. Made of lightweight stainless-steel tubes, it is remarkably strong and safe. This car has no roof or windshield, which makes helmets and weatherproof clothes essential at speed.

Monday morning: *invent car.* **Monday lunchtime:** *try to make car faster.* That's right, as soon as the car was invented we started trying to make it faster. Trouble is, there's more to driving than speed and power. A car needs to be able to *apply* all that lovely power in just the right way, otherwise you might as well use it to boil water. And that brings us to a word you'll read all the time in car magazines: handling.

Handling is all about making a car go along the road without sliding off into a field. Sliding off into fields wastes time, is pretty dangerous, and upsets cows.

To make a car handle well we need to get to grips with tires, suspension, weight, and we need to unravel the mysteries of understeer and oversteer (which are types of skid). And when you understand all these things and their relationship with science, you'll be a better driver. And, on the racing circuit, a quicker one.

Handling

ALL-terrain vehicle

Deserts, rivers, rocks, and mud—nothing stops a HMMWV (High Mobility Multipurpose Wheeled Vehicle, pronounced "humvee" or Hummer for short). Designed for military use over rough terrain, civilians can now buy smaller versions of the original aircraft-carrier-sized humvee. All Hummers have a low center of gravity, a powerful engine, and some clever technology to help them stay the right way up.

The Hummer was built for power and off-road agility. A V8 engine produces three times the horsepower of a family car, giving it superb climbing and scrambling ability.

Powerful gas-filled shock absorbers allow the wheels to rise and fall independently over bumps. Even if several wheels are stuck in mud or spinning in midair, the Hummer can still get itself out of trouble. It uses differential gears to redirect the engine torque away from the wheels that are stuck, feeding more to the wheels that can still grip—and so powers itself free.

The Hummer's self-leveling suspension system allows its wheels to tilt on bumpy ground while the body remains level.

Stability The center of gravity is the point inside an object where all its weight seems to be concentrated. Like anything else, cars tend to topple over if their center of gravity is too high or moves too much to one side. A Hummer is longer than a typical 4x4, with the wheels nearer the front and back, and it has a heavy, low engine. This squat design gives it a very low center of gravity. It can drive up, down, or sideways on slopes as long as its center of gravity stays inside the lines of stability (where its tires meet the ground).

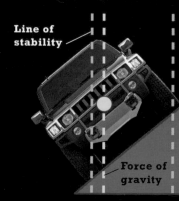

Line of stability

Force of gravity

40° side slope

Stable

Driving a Hummer on a 40° slope is easy. The car's massive, 3-ton weight acts down through the center of gravity, and since this is safely between the two lines of stability, there is no risk of toppling. The tires don't slip, thanks to chunky treads up to ½ in (13 mm) deep—at least 50 percent deeper than normal tires.

⬤ = car's center of gravity

No surface is too much for this all-action vehicle

Properly pumped-up tires help a car go quickly, safely, and save fuel. But in off-road mud, flatter, squishier tires give more grip and better handling. In a Hummer, the driver can pump the tires up or down automatically, to suit different terrain, using a switch on the dashboard.

With their engine air intakes high up the hood, Hummers can easily drive through shallow rivers. Military Hummers come with a snorkel that feeds air into the engine in water up to 5 ft (1.5 m) deep.

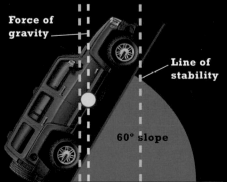

Force of gravity

Line of stability

60° slope

Stable

Driving forward, the Hummer can tackle slope angles up to 60°. With a heavy 6.2-liter engine at the front, the center of gravity lies safely toward the front of the car and within the lines of stability. Most 4x4 cars struggle to climb slopes steeper than 45°.

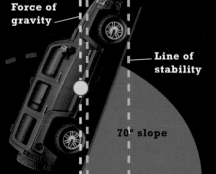

Force of gravity

Line of stability

Roll over

70° slope

Unstable

On a slightly steeper slope, the center of gravity is no longer between the lines of stability. Gravity will tend to tip the car backward, causing the car to roll.

MONSTER TRUCKS

Take a four-wheel-drive truck, beef up the engine, gearbox, and tires, reinforce the chassis, and add a sprinkling of science—and you get a monster truck: the kind of car that can **really** make a lasting impression.

Monster trucks regularly perform freestyle stunts, including wheelies, jumping, ...

This monster truck, Bigfoot, has tires 66 in (170 cm) in diameter and 43 in (110 cm) wide. By spreading the truck's 5 ton (4.5 metric ton) weight over a bigger area, huge tires reduce pressure on the ground, so the wheels can speed through thick mud.

... and car crushing.

Even though Bigfoot is three times heavier than a normal car, its supercharged, methanol-powered engine gives it a top speed of 70 mph (112 km/h). Driving up a ramp, it can use its momentum to clear 14 parked cars. One truck, Bigfoot 14, has even managed to jump over a Boeing 727 airliner.

Monster trucks get their amazing ability to climb cars and leap obstacles from their suspension. Massive tires, gigantic springs, and efficient shock absorbers all contribute to the suspension system. The same three parts are at work in all cars. Suspension systems act to keep the body of the car level when going over bumps by damping the vertical motion of the wheels.

Tires
Despite their huge size, Bigfoot's tires are not pumped to full pressure. This allows the rubber to deform around bumps in the surface, increasing the area in contact with the ground. Since the tires support the weight of the truck, spreading the force of impact over a larger area makes the tire less likely to burst when landing.

Tire

Spring
When a wheel hits a bump, the sturdy metal spring stretches or squeezes as the wheel moves up or down. Unless it is damped, the spring will keep bouncing up and down, because there's nowhere for the energy to go.

Spring

Shock absorber
A shock absorber, or damper, is a pump filled with gas that absorbs energy from the spring and transfers it to a piston. The piston pushes against the gas, which slows the piston down and turns its energy into heat.

Shock absorber

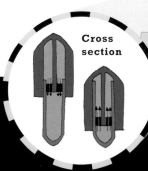

Cross section

Shock absorbers are speed sensitive—the faster the suspension moves, the more resistance the shock absorber provides.

...Keep on moving...

The science of inertia

Isaac Newton discovered a very important law about moving objects. He realized that once an object is moving, it likes to keep on moving in a straight line at a constant speed. And if it's not moving, it likes to stay still. This stubbornness has a scientific name: INERTIA. It's inertia that makes pools balls roll in straight lines, and it's inertia that makes shopping carts such a pain to steer, especially when they're full.

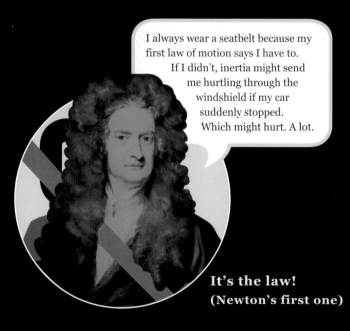

> I always wear a seatbelt because my first law of motion says I have to. If I didn't, inertia might send me hurtling through the windshield if my car suddenly stopped. Which might hurt. A lot.

It's the law!
(Newton's first one)

There's something odd about Newton's first law. Newton said that moving objects will continue in a straight line forever unless a force stops them, but common sense tells us that moving objects usually grind to a halt. That's because there usually *is* a force trying to stop them: the force of friction. Take away that (by going into space, for instance), and Newton's first law works rather well. In fact, it keeps all the stars, planets, and moons moving.

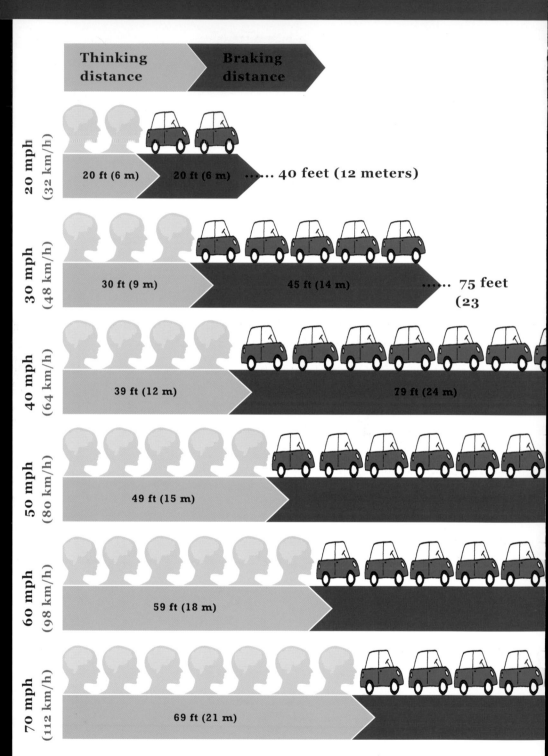

| Thinking distance | Braking distance |

Speed	Thinking distance	Braking distance	Total
20 mph (32 km/h)	20 ft (6 m)	20 ft (6 m)	40 feet (12 meters)
30 mph (48 km/h)	30 ft (9 m)	45 ft (14 m)	75 feet (23
40 mph (64 km/h)	39 ft (12 m)	79 ft (24 m)	
50 mph (80 km/h)	49 ft (15 m)		
60 mph (98 km/h)	59 ft (18 m)		
70 mph (112 km/h)	69 ft (21 m)		

Stopping distance

To stop a moving car, you have to overcome its inertia by using a force: friction from the brakes. The brakes get rid of the car's kinetic energy by turning it into heat energy and sound, but they are designed to do this gradually—otherwise the car would stop in an instant and *your* inertia would send you flying out of your seat. The faster a car is going, the more kinetic energy it has, and the longer the brakes take to stop it. The chart shows how far a car's inertia will carry it when a driver stops in an emergency. The total stopping distance has two parts: thinking distance (when the driver is reacting) and braking distance (when the driver has slammed his foot on the brakes).

■ ■ Why are cars such an effort to stop and start?

There's no escaping inertia ...

The only way to overcome inertia is to apply a force. You need a massive force to overcome the inertia of a standing car. But once the car's moving, inertia makes it easier to push.

You have to overcome inertia to make a car turn, otherwise it will keep going in a straight line. Tires use the force of friction to overcome inertia, but the passengers' inertia pushes them the other way.

Ever flown into the air when your car went over a bump? It was inertia that kept you and your car floating in the air for a moment before the force of gravity pulled you down.

As a car's speed rises, the braking distance leaps up by bigger and bigger increments. The world's fastest car—Thrust SSC—has a total stopping distance of 6 miles (10 km).

.... 118 feet (36 meters)

125 ft (38 m) .... 175 feet (53 meters)

180 ft (55 m) .... 240 feet (73 meters)

246 ft (75 m) .... 315 feet (96 meters)

Thinking time

Drivers need lightning-fast reactions to stay safe in an emergency. Most drivers take 0.7 seconds to respond to a sudden hazard, but this thinking time can more than triple if a person has consumed alcohol or if they're distracted by a cell phone. And that can add hundreds of feet to the stopping distance, making an accident far more likely.

Keep your head on

A Formula 1 driver's body fits snugly inside his car, but his head pokes out of the top of the cabin, and his heavy helmet adds to his head's inertia. In a high-speed crash, head + helmet try to keep moving forward after the car has stopped, straining the driver's neck as though his head weighed half a ton. This is not good for his neck. So as a precaution, Formula 1 drivers now bolt their heads to the car using a special "head and neck support system" (HANS).

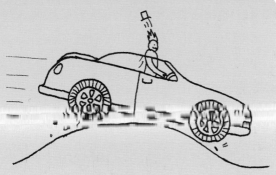

65

G-force

Imagine you're a Formula 1 driver. As your car hurtles around the track, accelerating and decelerating suddenly, and twisting violently around the bends, tremendous forces seem to be shoving your body back and forth or from side to side. This shoving is caused by inertia: your body is trying to obey Newton's first law and keep going in straight line at a constant speed, but the car won't let it. The result is a powerful force that feels like gravity acting in strange directions—like gravity gone crazy. We call it **G-force.**

3 G ### Acceleration
A Formula 1 car can accelerate from 0 to 60 mph (0–96 km/h) in less than two seconds. This phenomenal acceleration generates a G-force in the opposite direction and presses the driver into the back of his seat with a force three times his body weight.

← G-force

5 G ### Downforce
When the car hits top speed along the straights, aerodynamic effects create up to 5 G of downforce, ramming the car's tires down onto the road. But this isn't the same as G-force, and the driver feels no downward force on his body.

Downforce ↓

What's the maximum G-force a person can take? That's the question that the brave (or crazy) scientist John Stapp tried to answer in 1954 when he strapped himself into an insanely dangerous rocket-powered train sled and then decelerated from 630 mph (1,017 km/h) to zero in 1.25 seconds, generating 46 G. He briefly weighed 3 tons and his eyes filled with blood—but he survived.

4 G **Cornering**
In the bends, inertia tries to make the driver go in a straight line, so he feels a G-force pushing him outward with up to four times his weight. The bucket seat holds him tight, but he must strain against the force to keep his head straight and his hands on the steering wheel.

G-force

6 G **Braking**
The carbon brakes used in Formula 1 are unbelievably powerful. They cause such violent deceleration that the driver is thrust forward by 6 G—the kind of G-force a fighter pilot regularly has to endure. The force squeezes tears from the driver's eyes and splatters his visor.

G-force

G-force limits

−3 G
The maximum negative G-force a person can take. Negative Gs push blood up into the brain and can burst blood vessels

Zero G
Weightlessness in space

1 G
Normal gravity

3 G
The maximum G-force experienced at the bottom of a hill on a big roller coaster

4.3 G
The maximum G-force that civilian aircraft are built to withstand

5 G
The point at which most people black out if G-force is sustained

The G-force generated by top dragsters during maximum acceleration

9 G
The maximum G-force that fighter pilots are trained to withstand during aerial maneuvers

46 G
The maximum G-force deliberately endured by a human being

100 G
Exposure to 100 G is almost always fatal, however brief

180 G
The maximum G-force a human being has survived

In the HOT seat

What's it like to drive a Formula 1 car?

Extremely difficult. What's it like to compete in a Formula 1 race? Almost impossible. F1 cars are blindingly fast and incredibly sensitive to the driver's controls, which makes lightning-fast reactions and supreme concentration essential. Yet the driver must battle continually with violent G-forces, sweltering heat, and deafening noise—all of which makes competing in Formula 1 as physically exhausting as running a marathon.

Mental training is just as important for F1 drivers as physical—no other sport demands such intense concentration. Drivers train with psychologists to ensure they have unwavering mind control during the race. They memorize maps and visualize the perfect lap, so that when they arrive at the track they feel like they've driven it many times before.

THE STEERING WHEEL gives the driver control of everything except acceleration and braking, so he need never take his hands off. Gears are changed by flappy paddles, and the small buttons control a host of functions (many kept secret) from traction control to a drinks dispenser—drinks are pumped by tube straight to the driver's mouth.

Ferrari 2008 steering wheel

IN THE COCKPIT

Drivers sit so close to the ground that they sometimes get heat blisters on their backsides. The car has very little suspension, which means drivers feel every bump in the road—and painfully. Knee and ankle protectors can help prevent the inevitable bruises caused by violent jolts to the car.

F1 cars have tailor-made "bucket seats" molded to a cast of the driver's body. The seat must hold the driver snugly to prevent G-force from throwing him sideways. A tough six-part harness keeps the driver tightly strapped in. Without this, he'd be thrown from the car when braking suddenly.

Harness

OUCH!

The faster an object hurtles around, the more powerful the force. To stay on the wall of death, the car has to go fast enough for centrifugal force to push its tires firmly against the wall—only then will the tires create enough friction to grip the surface and resist the pull of gravity. If the car slows down, gravity wins out and the car will tumble off and smash to the ground. At this wall of death in India, it looks like a few planks have been taken by spectators—which could have some unfortunate consequences.

FRICTION vs. INERTIA:
The science of skids

A car's tires fight a never-ending battle against its inertia. Cars want to move in straight lines at constant speed (thank Newton's first law), but the tires must use the force of friction to grip the road and push the car around bends, overcoming inertia. Most of the time they win the battle, but sometimes they lose. And when that happens, tires lose their grip and slide screeching across the tarmac—the car has gone into a *skid*. Skids are involved in quarter of all crashes, so knowing how to regain control is a matter of life and death.

FRONT-WHEEL SKID (UNDERSTEER)

Help! I can't turn sharply enough!

What happens: Front wheels lose grip and the car fails to turn as sharply as it should.
Cause: Driving too fast while turning or braking too hard while turning.
Remedy: Remove the cause by taking your foot off the accelerator or brake pedal. If possible, straighten the steering momentarily.

What happens: Rear wheels lose their grip, causing the back of the car to swinga round.
Cause: Accelerating around a corner or sudden braking in a rear-wheel-drive car.
Remedy: Remove the cause by taking your foot off the accelerator or brake and turning the steering wheel in the opposite way.

REAR-WHEEL SKID (OVERSTEER)

*Now I'm turning **too** sharply!!!*

What causes skids?

Skids happen when the force of friction under the tires is overcome by a more powerful force. A sharp turn, sudden acceleration, or heavy braking can all induce forces powerful enough to overcome grip. If the road is wet or icy, friction is much weaker and skids are far more likely to happen. On very wet roads, a wedge of water can build up in front of the tire and then lift it slightly off the road, causing the car to skate uncontrollably. This is called aquaplaning.

Normal

Aquaplaning

FOUl -WHEEL SKID

Now I'm not turning at all! Aaarrgghh!!

What happens: All four wheels lose grip, causing the car to slide in a straight line like a shopping cart.
Cause: Sudden braking in wet or icy conditions.
Remedy: Press the brakes firmly, but if the wheels lock up, momentarily release the brakes and press again.

Regaining control of a skidding car can be a bit hairy, not to mention dangerous. So a better strategy is to avoid skidding in the first place. Modern cars now come equipped with cunning gadgets that can detect the first sign of a skid by monitoring the wheels. If some wheels start spinning much faster or slower than others, they've lost grip and could cause a skid.

Traction control systems use sensors to monitor the turning speed of the wheels. If one of the driven wheels (the ones that the engine is driving) is turning much faster than the others, it must have lost grip. The traction control computer spots this and either cuts the engine power briefly, applies the brakes, or both.

Antilock braking systems (ABS) come into play if a wheel stops turning—a sign that the brake has "locked" the wheel, which can happen on wet or icy roads. The system automatically releases and reapplies the brake in short bursts, allowing the wheel to roll and so regain its grip of the road.

Brake

Electronic stability program (ESP) uses information from sensors to detect when the car is about to skid and then applies braking force to one or more wheels to correct it, while also reducing engine power. It's an excellent safety system and all cars should have it. Within a few years they will.

Losing your grip

Skids can be pretty scary when they catch you unawares. For a second or two, you lose control of the car and may find yourself watching helplessly as you career gracefully off the road in a completely unexpected direction, wondering where you might end up. So it might come as a surprise to learn that skilled drivers often induce skids deliberately—sometimes just for the thrill of it, and sometimes to enable tricky maneuvers. Here are a few tricks of the trade. Oh, and **DON'T** try these at home.

POWERSLIDING

A powerslide is a deliberate rear-wheel skid. The easiest way to do it is to step hard on the accelerator in a rear-wheel drive car while turning sharply. The sudden burst of power at the rear wheels causes them to spin and lose grip in the turn, with the result that the back of the car swings out sideways rather than following the front into the turn. The driver then turns the steering wheel into the skid so that the car slides sideways, with the rear wheels still skidding and the front wheels rolling. There are several other ways of inducing powerslides, but all of them work the same way, causing loss of traction at the rear.

HANDBRAKE TURN

By using the handbrake to lock the rear wheels and so destroy their grip, a driver can swing a car through 180° in a tight space and shoot off in the opposite direction. Handy for chases.

DOUGHNUT

The idea here is simply to spin a car around and around wildly with the wheels at one or both ends skidding. If the tires screech, smoke, and make a doughnut pattern of skid marks, so much the better. Ideal for causing injuries, noise, and damage to cars or property. Not much use otherwise, though some race-car-driving drivers cata fans with victory doughnuts after winning races.

BURNOUT

This means spinning the rear wheels while a car is standing or moving slowly, and it usually involves a lot of noise and smoke. Handy in drag racing, where it provides a quick means of heating the tires, which in turn provides maximum grip.

FISHTAILING

Fishtailing happens by accident when rear-wheel drive cars lose grip at the rear in a turn and swing around. The driver tries to correct the skid with steering but overdoes it, causing the tail to flick the other way (like a fish). If the driver fails to regain control, the swings get worse until the car spins out of control.

J-TURN

This is a little like a handbrake turn, except that the car starts off reversing rapidly and then swings through a tight half-turn to point forward, before racing away. Perfect for a rapid getaway, and often seen done by stunt-drivers in films. Although it looks and sounds more exciting if the tires squeal and burn, no skidding is needed—just quick reactions and good control. Think of it as a turbocharged version of reverse parking.

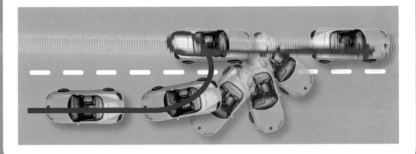

PIT maneuver

How do you stop a speeding car? US police departments use the Pursuit Intervention Technique. The police driver drives beside the car being pursued but holds back slightly to align the front of his car with the rear of the suspect's car. Then he turns sharply to ram the side of the suspect's car and make its rear wheels break from the road and lose grip, causing a fishtail.

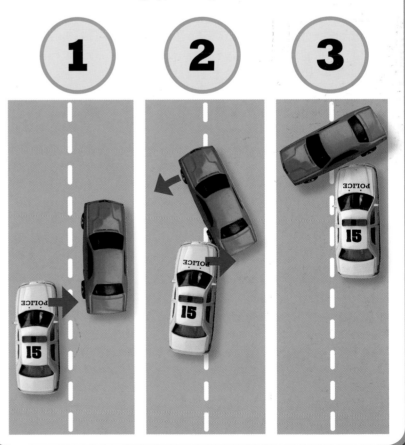

Car-CRasH science

When a car hits another object at speed, something has to give. Cars can be designed to survive crashes without a scratch—but **we need to survive** them, too.

It takes forces to make things move and forces to stop them. To stop something gradually and gently, a small force is enough—think of the light touch on the brakes that can gradually slow a bike down. But to stop something very suddenly, you need a much larger force.

You can make a car accelerate from 0–60 mph (0–100 km/h) in 5–10 seconds. But in a car crash, you can go from 60–0 in less than a second. You feel massive force when a car speeds up. You might feel 100 times more force when you crash because the deceleration happens so quickly.

Triple whammy

If you could study a car crash in slow-motion, you'd discover that there are actually three separate impacts (right). Each impact involves sudden deceleration, and that creates deadly forces. The secret to making cars safe is to *slow down* each impact, which prolongs the deceleration and therefore reduces the forces. Slowing down the impact by a fraction of a second can be enough to save lives.

1st impact
Car hits obstacle

2nd impact
Body hits inside of car (or would if there weren't an airbag)

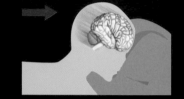

3rd impact
Brain hits skull (and may rebound to hit back of skull too)

Crumple zones

At the front and rear of a car are "crumple zones"—areas deliberately designed to crumple up like an accordion in a collision. This slows down the car's deceleration and thereby dramatically reduces the impact forces. Just 3 ft (1 m) of crumpled car can cut the forces reaching the passengers by 90 percent.

crasH

Built like us...

Head
Contains three force sensors to measure impacts on brain.

Neck
Has nine sensors and pulleys inside so it can move in any direction to measure whiplash.

Chest
Rib sensors measure impacts from seat belts or the steering wheel column.

Legs
Force sensors in the pelvis, thigh, knee, and ankles assess likelihood of fractures and dislocations of joints.

Skin
Steel and aluminum structure is covered with foam and vinyl to simulate skin puncture impacts.

Crash test dummies

They don't call them dummies for nothing. Well, would you sit in a car that was just about to crash? Once, engineers used dead bodies to test cars. Now they use plastic people, costing over $200,000, instead. They might look silly, but they're pretty smart inside. They're packed with 130 different sensors—concentrated in the head, chest, and upper leg (the parts most likely to get hurt). The bodies are weighted and jointed like real bodies: in a crash, the arms flail about and the head swings violently forward, just like the real thing. With computers recording everything the dummies feel, engineers know exactly what injuries people could get— and how to avoid them.

Believe it or not, some car colors appear to be much safer than others. A study in New Zealand in the late 1990s found that you're more likely to have a crash if you drive a brown car rather than a silver one. But is this because silver cars are safer or because safe drivers prefer the color silver? Or can they just be seen more easily?

The passenger safety cage is a rigid steel cell between the front and back crumple zones. Designed to stay the same shape even in a severe crash or rollover, it stops passengers from getting squashed or trapped as the car changes shape. Impact energy is safely deflected around the passengers by the cage bars.

Airbags let the passengers stop more slowly than the car. When the airbag sensor detects a large deceleration (a sudden stop), the bags inflate in less than a twentieth of a second, giving a much softer impact than the steering wheel. Stopping the passenger more slowly means less force—and less damage.

Help! This is going to hurt.

Seatbelts improve your chance of surviving a crash by 50–75 percent, mainly by preventing inertia from throwing you through the windshield. They also spread the force of impact over a larger area of your body, making injuries less severe. They stretch too, slowing you down more slowly so your body feels less force.

Size matters—when a car hits a truck, you're less likely to be injured if you're in the truck. It has more mass and energy, so it's harder to stop because its momentum continues to carry it forward. As it thumps the car, it transfers a huge amount of energy— and that's what does the damage.

The gasoline engine

has ruled the world of cars for more than a century, but things may be about to change. Scientists and engineers are working nonstop to come up with new technologies that do less harm to the environment, and the ideas they're working on will lead to some fantastic new cars. It's very exciting stuff.

Remember the first electric cars from the 1860s? They weren't very good because their batteries were heavy and went flat quickly. Well, the electric cars heading our way not only have much better batteries but also deliver supercar performance, while being as quiet as a mouse and a joy to drive. And there's lots more in the pipeline, from flying cars to cars that go under water—so turn the page for a glimpse into the future.

Technology

What's it MADE of ?

Animal, vegetable, and mineral

A car is composed of elements from each of the three classifications—animal, vegetable, and mineral. The metals, originating in the last of the trio, provide by far the greatest overall contribution to a typical steel-bodied car.

0.5% cow

Leather is used for the seating and interior trim in some cars.

+

5% tree

Trees provide rubber for tires and wood for steering wheels and trim.

Steel and aluminum

A steel chassis is usually made from a number of pressings that are then welded together. If you make the parts from aluminum instead, you halve their weight. Every piece of aluminum used to lighten a car cuts fuel consumption—over the lifetime of the vehicle, this saves at least **20 times** its weight in carbon dioxide emissions from entering the atmosphere.

Aluminum

Steel

Kevlar

When a car brakes, its pads create so much friction that they can heat to over 930°F (500°C)! Modern brake pads are made from heatproof materials including metals, ceramics, carbon fibers, and composites based on Kevlar. Kevlar is a synthetic fiber that is five times stronger than steel and is also used to make bulletproof vests.

Carbon fiber and plastic

This Porsche incorporates carbon-fiber-reinforced plastic for its body parts, instead of steel or aluminum. The plastic body is molded in a single piece to create a monocoque design. This makes the car especially rigid and strong.

Alloys

If you run a car engine at moderate speed for an hour a day, the pistons will pump up and down **75 million** times in a year. Pistons are usually cast from strong, light, aluminum-silicon alloys. The silicon stops the aluminum from expanding as much, so the piston fits better at a wider range of temperatures. Allowing fuel to burn more cleanly in the cylinders, and so, the engine creates less pollution. ■

Plastics

Until the early 1980s, most cars had steel bumpers "plated" with shiny chrome, but they were easy to dent. The solution was plastic—it became popular since it was strong, light, and easy to mold. Some new cars have bumpers made from extralight and strong nanocomposites—plastics mixed with enhancing substances.

Titanium

A strong, light aerospace metal similar to aluminum, titanium is used to reduce weight in cars like the Chevrolet Corvette, which has its exhaust made from the metal. Although not rare, titanium costs a lot to process and is much more expensive than aluminum, which tends to be used instead.

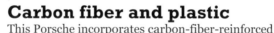

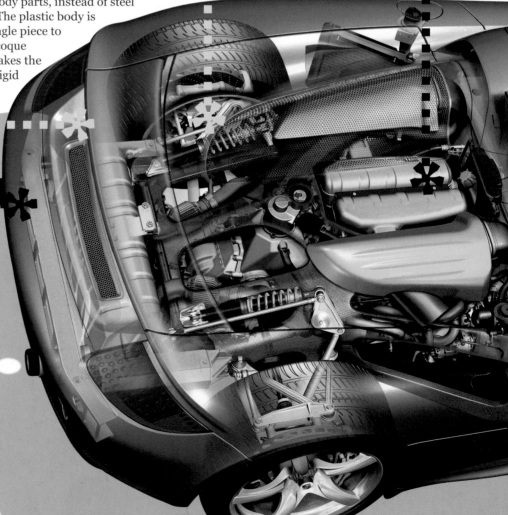

When people say cars are **"lumps of metal,"** they're wrong on both counts. A modern car is built with the same attention to detail as a **jet plane** or a **space rocket**—from literally dozens of different materials that are chosen to make the car operate as efficiently as possible.

+ 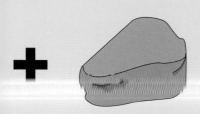 **82.5% rock**
Iron ore creates the steel for a car's bodywork, engine, and wheels. Sand is used to make glass.

+  **12% oil**
Oil is used to produce the plastics found in a car's interior and some engine components.

= **100% car**

Leather Car seats evolved from leather horse saddles, which is why luxury cars still have leather interiors today. Plastic is more common in cheaper models. Carmakers have tried other materials, too— the 1965 Mercer-Cobra had a copper-lined interior.

Laminates Car windshields are made of a laminate "sandwich" composed from two sheets of glass on the outside with a plastic layer in between. If a stone breaks the outer glass, the impact spreads outward, and the screen smashes into tiny nuggets. These are less dangerous than larger, sharper pieces.

Platinum
The catalytic converter is the pollution filter in a car's exhaust pipe. It is made from a ceramic honeycomb coated with precious metals such as platinum, which costs about $22,000 per pound ($50,000 per kilogram). Gram for gram, the metal in the catalytic converter is the most expensive material in a car. If the whole vehicle were made from platinum, it would cost over $100,000,000!

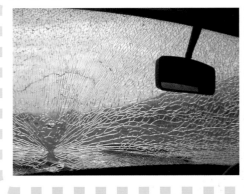

Polycarbonates Lights and indicators are covered with shatterproof plastic called polycarbonate. The ridged lines you see on the plastic bend light like the lens used in a lighthouse, focusing the beam tightly on the road.

Alloys When carts became chariots, solid wooden wheels were replaced by lightweight frames of spokes. Modern car wheels have gone down a similar road. Instead of a heavy steel hub, sports cars have lighter, faster wheels with spokes cast from a single piece of superstrong aluminum or magnesium alloy. Alloy wheels are lighter, helping to reduce the car's weight and improve its handling.

Rubber A modern tire is made from lots of different ingredients. About 40 percent of it is vulcanized (cooked and chemically treated) rubber, which provides grip and a smooth ride. Just under a third is material to make the rubber go further. Another 15 percent is reinforcing materials (steel, nylon, and rayon) to make the tire stronger. The rest is made from enhancing chemical additives. Though tires can be recycled, one billion are thrown away each year—enough to stretch to the Moon and back.

Electric dreams

Zap! Electric cars are on the way, with unbelievable acceleration, 100% torque, near-silent motors, and no exhaust—let alone emissions. Could these supercars save the planet? Or is there a catch?

There's no engine in an electric car such as the Tesla Roadster. Instead, an electric motor drives the wheels. This set-up has big advantages:

✔ The motor provides 100% torque whatever the revs, providing supercar acceleration.

✔ There's no need for fuel—just plug in to recharge.

✔ Electric cars are cheap to run. The Tesla does the equivalent to 135 miles (217 km) per gallon.

✔ No exhaust fumes or emissions.

✔ Because the powertrain has only a handful of moving parts, the car needs almost no maintenance.

The Tesla Roadster is no battery-powered toy. It may be powered by laptop batteries (6,831 of them, to be precise) but its electric motor can accelerate the car from 0 to 60 mph (97 km/h) in 4 seconds and take it to a top speed of 125 mph (200 km/h)—yet it barely makes a sound. In fact, electric cars are so quiet that artificial *vroom* sounds have to be added so people can hear them coming.

The main drawback with electric cars is the batteries. The Tesla's lithium-ion battery pack weighs nearly half a ton but can only store as much energy as about 2 gallons (8 liters) of gas. That's still enough to take you 220 miles (354 km), but then you have to stop and recharge. Which takes 3½ hours. And although the car does not *directly* pollute the air with CO_2 or other emissions, the power plant that supplied the electricity may well have used fossil fuels.

Coming soon...

Whizz-wheels

Tomorrow's electric cars could do away with the engine compartment altogether. This ELIICA (Electric LIthium-Ion Car) has a tiny battery-powered electric motor built into each wheel hub. Eight hub motors give eight times the power and a top speed of over 230 mph (370 km/h).

Wheelie far

Electric cars probably make you think of battery-powered toys that conk out when the batteries die. This sporty Mitsubishi hub-motor car couldn't be more different. It can do 125 miles (200 km) on a single charge and has a top speed of 80 mph (130 km/h). It even has solar panels on the roof.